THIS TEA JOURNAL
BELONGS TO:

_____

IF FOUND, PLEASE RETURN TO:

ADDRESS _____

PHONE_____
E-MAIL

TABLE OF CONTENTS

Tea Journal
A Tea Lover's Diary

Capturing Moments of Joy
At Tea Shops, Tea Rooms and Tea Parties

Jennifer C. Petersen

This book or any portion thereof may not be reproduced or used in any manner whatsoever without the express written permission of the publisher except for the use of brief quotations in a book review.

Disclaimer and Terms of Use:

The Author and Publisher has strived to be as accurate and complete as possible in the creation of this book, notwithstanding the fact that she does not warrant or represent at any time that the contents within are accurate due to the rapidly changing nature of the contents and the Internet. While all attempts have been made to verify information provided in this publication, the Author and Publisher assume no responsibility for errors, omissions, or contrary interpretation of the subject matter herein. Any perceived slights of specific persons, people, or organization are unintentional.

Printed in the United States of America.

First Printing, 2014
Library of Congress Control Number: 2014932261

Tea Trade Mart Publishing
800 NE Tenney Rd 110-429
Vancouver, WA 98685
www.jenniferpetersen.com

TEA MUSINGS

As I think about tea room visits over the years, many places come to mind. From the types of tea served to the interior ambiance, each holds a special memory. Each one was somewhat different much as their proprietors' personalities differed.

From the Ritz-Carlton and Intercontinental Hotel to the Perennial Tea Room and Cheshire Cat, each tea service has been unique in one way or another. Sometimes, it's the little things that count like the smell of cookies from the kitchen or the teapot clad in a quilted tea cozy.

The tea at the Cheshire Cat was always Yorkshire Red or Gold teabags and served piping hot. Avril Massey, now retired, had made so many pots of tea in her lifetime that she could work miracles with a teabag. It was delicious! Avril retired years ago but the memory of her shop is always present.

The first time I visited the Perennial Tea Room in Post Alley at Pike's Place Market in Seattle, I immediately saw a wide selection of loose-leaf teas available. It was such a nice place that I decided to stay for lunch only to learn that they don't serve "afternoon tea". Note to self: never assume how service should be offered at a "tea shop" or "tea room". It was suggested that I choose a tea accompanied by a packet of lavender shortbread from their gift shop area. Whether it was the atmosphere or the time of day, it was the best tea and shortbread in the world!

One of the best places for photo ops is Myrtle's Tea House in Ridgefield, WA. The tables are space apart adequately for privacy, the interior is well-suited to photo backdrops and the tea plates are perfectly arranged. I puzzle over how the owner can take a simple pot of tea and present it with such style and grace.

At the Ritz-Carlton, as much as I enjoy the tea service, I doubly enjoy reading the tea menu, the near silent service, the occasional clink of spoon against teacup, and the elegant surroundings. Moreover, one never knows when a diplomat or royalty may be seated nearby.

The guest service is so exemplary in every way at Peet's Coffee and Tea that I always end up buying tin of tea or tea accessory – as though I need another box of tea in the cabinet.

With all due respect to those who desire perfection in all things related to tea, to me if the tea is excellent and service is friendly, I'm happy.

We each have our own criteria for the perfect tea experience. I'll venture to say that if all of us went to the same tea establishments, our Tea Journals would be as different as we are.

Do you save samples of your loose-leaf teas? Do you keep the tea bag envelope? Do you take photos of the entrance, interior and companions?

Then keep a tea journal and rate your experiences.

On the following pages, there is plenty of space to write your thoughts on one page and attach photos, illustrations, and tea menu or tea tasting notes to the other page.

Raising my teacup to you!

Jennifer

TEACUP RATING

OVERALL RATING: 1 - 5 TEACUPS WITH 5 BEING EXCEPTIONAL.

RATING YOUR EXPERIENCE BY TEACUPS

The tea review icons are a good reference for your overall perception of your experience for later reference.

Questions to ask yourself before scoring your tea review:

1) Was the interior clean and free of clutter? Were tables cleaned between guest seatings including fresh china, cutlery, napkins and menus?

2) Were the restrooms fresh, clean and nicely decorated? Were they well stocked with plenty of toilet paper, soap and single-use towels?

3) Were the teacups, cutlery and other service ware in good condition and appropriate sizes?

4) Was the staff friendly, attentive and knowledgeable? Were you acknowledged and greeted with a smile upon arrival and departure?

5) Was service efficient and attentive? Did the staff explain the menu and quantities precisely?

6) Were the baked goods or other foods freshly prepared?

7) Was there a specialty tea menu listing loose-leaf teas available? Was the staff well-trained and able to answer questions about the teas? Was the tea prepared correctly and to your satisfaction? Was the water fresh, non-chlorinated and at the correct temperature for each tea?

8) Was the overall experience one of luxury as well as good value?

9) Tea preparation: tea experts generally consider the following for correctly infused tea:

  a. preparation
  b. service
  c. tea liquor appearance
  d. water temperature
  e. taste

    The 4 T's of tea making: type, temperature, time, taste

IDEAS FOR TEA JOURNAL:

For each tea place visited, write the name on the corresponding page line in the Table of Contents.

Tea notes:
    Name
    Brand
    Type (white, green, oolong, black, flavored)
    Added milk, sugar and/or lemon?
    Overall flavor

Menu notes:
    Menu selection?
    Menu chosen
    On the next visit, I want to try _____.
    Special recipes?
    Tea and food paired well?
    Tea and food presented attractively?

Photos allowed? Photo permission needed?
    Photos of tea.
    Photos of table setting or interior.
    Photo of you with your companions.
    Photo of you with the proprietor.

Comments about transportation or parking?

Things you loved best!

TEA PLACE 1 _____

Scrapbook Memories

Tea Views 1

Teacup Rating

OVERALL RATING: 1 - 5 TEACUPS WITH 5 BEING EXCEPTIONAL.

*D*ate ___ / / ___

*T*ea *S*hop _____

*P*roprietor _____

*L*ocation _____

*C*ompanions _____

*T*ea *N*ames and *T*ypes _____

*T*ea *T*asting *N*otes _____

_____

*M*enu *N*otes _____

_____

*P*roprietor's *A*utograph _____

TEA PLACE 2 _____

Scrapbook Memories

TEA VIEWS 2

TEACUP RATING

1 2 3 4 5

OVERALL RATING: 1 - 5 TEACUPS WITH 5 BEING EXCEPTIONAL.

Date _____/ /_____

Tea Shop _____

Proprietor _____

Location _____

Companions _____

Tea Names and Types _____

Tea Tasting Notes _____

_____

Menu Notes _____

_____

Proprietor's Autograph _____

TEA PLACE 3 _____

Scrapbook Memories

TEA VIEWS 3

TEACUP RATING

1 2 3 4 5

OVERALL RATING: 1 - 5 TEACUPS WITH 5 BEING EXCEPTIONAL.

*D*ate ___/___/___

*T*ea *S*hop _____

*P*roprietor _____

*L*ocation _____

*C*ompanions _____

*T*ea *N*ames and *T*ypes _____

*T*ea *T*asting *N*otes _____

_____

*M*enu *N*otes _____

_____

*P*roprietor's *A*utograph _____

TEA PLACE 4 _____

Scrapbook Memories

TEA VIEWS 4

TEACUP RATING

1 2 3 4 5

$\mathcal{D}_{ate}$ ___/___/___

OVERALL RATING: 1 - 5 TEACUPS WITH 5 BEING EXCEPTIONAL.

$\mathcal{T}_{ea} \mathcal{S}_{hop}$ _____

$\mathcal{P}_{roprietor}$ _____

$\mathcal{L}_{ocation}$ _____

$\mathcal{C}_{ompanions}$ _____

$\mathcal{T}_{ea} \mathcal{N}_{ames and} \mathcal{T}_{ypes}$ _____

$\mathcal{T}_{ea} \mathcal{T}_{asting} \mathcal{N}_{otes}$ _____

_____

$\mathcal{M}_{enu} \mathcal{N}_{otes}$ _____

_____

$\mathcal{P}_{roprietor's} \mathcal{A}_{utograph}$ _____

TEA PLACE 5 _____

Scrapbook Memories

TEA VIEWS 5

TEACUP RATING

1   2   3   4   5

OVERALL RATING: 1 - 5 TEACUPS WITH 5 BEING EXCEPTIONAL.

Date ___/___/___

Tea Shop _____

Proprietor _____

Location _____

Companions _____

Tea Names and Types _____

Tea Tasting Notes _____

_____

Menu Notes _____

_____

Proprietor's Autograph _____

TEA PLACE 6 _____

Scrapbook Memories

TEA VIEWS 6

TEACUP RATING

1 2 3 4 5

OVERALL RATING: 1 - 5 TEACUPS WITH 5 BEING EXCEPTIONAL.

$\mathcal{D}$ate _____ / / _____

$\mathcal{T}$ea $\mathcal{S}$hop _____

$\mathcal{P}$roprietor _____

$\mathcal{L}$ocation _____

$\mathcal{C}$ompanions _____

$\mathcal{T}$ea $\mathcal{N}$ames and $\mathcal{T}$ypes _____

$\mathcal{T}$ea $\mathcal{T}$asting $\mathcal{N}$otes _____

_____

$\mathcal{M}$enu $\mathcal{N}$otes _____

_____

$\mathcal{P}$roprietor's $\mathcal{A}$utograph _____

TEA PLACE 7 _____

Scrapbook Memories

TEA VIEWS 7

TEACUP RATING

1   2   3   4   5

OVERALL RATING: 1 - 5 TEACUPS WITH 5 BEING EXCEPTIONAL.

Date _____ / / _____

Tea Shop _____

Proprietor _____

Location _____

Companions _____

Tea Names and Types _____

Tea Tasting Notes _____

_____

Menu Notes _____

_____

Proprietor's Autograph _____

TEA PLACE 8 _____

Scrapbook Memories

TEA VIEWS 8

TEACUP RATING

1 2 3 4 5

OVERALL RATING: 1 - 5 TEACUPS WITH 5 BEING EXCEPTIONAL.

Date __/__/____

Tea Shop _____

Proprietor _____

Location _____

Companions _____

Tea Names and Types _____

Tea Tasting Notes _____

_____

Menu Notes _____

_____

Proprietor's Autograph _____

TEA PLACE 9 _____

Scrapbook Memories

TEA VIEWS 9

TEACUP RATING

1 2 3 4 5

OVERALL RATING: 1 - 5 TEACUPS WITH 5 BEING EXCEPTIONAL.

Date ___/___/___

Tea Shop _____

Proprietor _____

Location _____

Companions _____

Tea Names and Types _____

Tea Tasting Notes _____

_____

Menu Notes _____

_____

Proprietor's Autograph _____

TEA PLACE 10 _____

Scrapbook Memories

TEA VIEWS 10

TEACUP RATING

1 2 3 4 5

OVERALL RATING: 1 - 5 TEACUPS WITH 5 BEING EXCEPTIONAL.

$\mathcal{D}$ate ___/___/___

$\mathcal{T}$ea $\mathcal{S}$hop _____

$\mathcal{P}$roprietor _____

$\mathcal{L}$ocation _____

$\mathcal{C}$ompanions _____

$\mathcal{T}$ea $\mathcal{N}$ames and $\mathcal{T}$ypes _____

$\mathcal{T}$ea $\mathcal{T}$asting $\mathcal{N}$otes _____

_____

$\mathcal{M}$enu $\mathcal{N}$otes _____

_____

$\mathcal{P}$roprietor's $\mathcal{A}$utograph _____

TEA PLACE 11 _____

Scrapbook Memories

TEA VIEWS 11

TEACUP RATING

1   2   3   4   5

$\mathcal{D}$ate ___ / / ___

OVERALL RATING: 1 - 5 TEACUPS WITH 5 BEING EXCEPTIONAL.

$\mathcal{T}$ea $\mathcal{S}$hop ___

$\mathcal{P}$roprietor ___

$\mathcal{L}$ocation ___

$\mathcal{C}$ompanions ___

$\mathcal{T}$ea $\mathcal{N}$ames and $\mathcal{T}$ypes ___

$\mathcal{T}$ea $\mathcal{T}$asting $\mathcal{N}$otes ___

___

$\mathcal{M}$enu $\mathcal{N}$otes ___

___

$\mathcal{P}$roprietor's $\mathcal{A}$utograph ___

TEA PLACE 12 _____

Scrapbook Memories

TEA VIEWS 12

TEACUP RATING

1 2 3 4 5

OVERALL RATING: 1 - 5 TEACUPS WITH 5 BEING EXCEPTIONAL.

$\mathcal{D}$ate ___/___/___

$\mathcal{T}$ea $\mathcal{S}$hop _____

$\mathcal{P}$roprietor _____

$\mathcal{L}$ocation _____

$\mathcal{C}$ompanions _____

$\mathcal{T}$ea $\mathcal{N}$ames and $\mathcal{T}$ypes _____

$\mathcal{T}$ea $\mathcal{T}$asting $\mathcal{N}$otes _____

_____

$\mathcal{M}$enu $\mathcal{N}$otes _____

_____

$\mathcal{P}$roprietor's $\mathcal{A}$utograph _____

TEA PLACE 13 _____

Scrapbook Memories

TEA VIEWS 13

TEACUP RATING

| 1 | 2 | 3 | 4 | 5 |

OVERALL RATING: 1 - 5 TEACUPS WITH 5 BEING EXCEPTIONAL.

$\mathcal{D}$ate ___ / ___ / ___

$\mathcal{T}$ea $\mathcal{S}$hop _____

$\mathcal{P}$roprietor _____

$\mathcal{L}$ocation _____

$\mathcal{C}$ompanions _____

$\mathcal{T}$ea $\mathcal{N}$ames and $\mathcal{T}$ypes _____

$\mathcal{T}$ea $\mathcal{T}$asting $\mathcal{N}$otes _____

_____

$\mathcal{M}$enu $\mathcal{N}$otes _____

_____

$\mathcal{P}$roprietor's $\mathcal{A}$utograph _____

TEA PLACE 14 _____

Scrapbook Memories

TEA VIEWS 14

TEACUP RATING

1   2   3   4   5

OVERALL RATING: 1 - 5 TEACUPS WITH 5 BEING EXCEPTIONAL.

$\mathcal{D}$ate   /   /

$\mathcal{T}$ea $\mathcal{S}$hop

$\mathcal{P}$roprietor

$\mathcal{L}$ocation

$\mathcal{C}$ompanions

$\mathcal{T}$ea $\mathcal{N}$ames and $\mathcal{T}$ypes

$\mathcal{T}$ea $\mathcal{T}$asting $\mathcal{N}$otes

$\mathcal{M}$enu $\mathcal{N}$otes

$\mathcal{P}$roprietor's $\mathcal{A}$utograph

TEA PLACE 15 _____

Scrapbook Memories

TEA VIEWS 15

TEACUP RATING

1 2 3 4 5

Date _/_/_

OVERALL RATING: 1 - 5 TEACUPS WITH 5 BEING EXCEPTIONAL.

Tea Shop

Proprietor

Location

Companions

Tea Names and Types

Tea Tasting Notes

Menu Notes

Proprietor's Autograph

TEA PLACE 16 _____

Scrapbook Memories

TEA VIEWS 16

TEACUP RATING

1 2 3 4 5

Date / /

OVERALL RATING: 1 - 5 TEACUPS WITH 5 BEING EXCEPTIONAL.

Tea Shop

Proprietor

Location

Companions

Tea Names and Types

Tea Tasting Notes

Menu Notes

Proprietor's Autograph

TEA PLACE 17 _____

Scrapbook Memories

TEA VIEWS 17

TEACUP RATING

1 2 3 4 5

$\mathcal{D}$ate _/ /_

OVERALL RATING: 1 - 5 TEACUPS WITH 5 BEING EXCEPTIONAL.

$\mathcal{T}$ea $\mathcal{S}$hop

$\mathcal{P}$roprietor

$\mathcal{L}$ocation

$\mathcal{C}$ompanions

$\mathcal{T}$ea $\mathcal{N}$ames and $\mathcal{T}$ypes

$\mathcal{T}$ea $\mathcal{T}$asting $\mathcal{N}$otes

$\mathcal{M}$enu $\mathcal{N}$otes

$\mathcal{P}$roprietor's $\mathcal{A}$utograph

TEA PLACE 18 _____

Scrapbook Memories

TEA VIEWS 18

TEACUP RATING

OVERALL RATING: 1 - 5 TEACUPS WITH 5 BEING EXCEPTIONAL.

Date ___ / / _____

Tea Shop _____

Proprietor _____

Location _____

Companions _____

Tea Names and Types _____

Tea Tasting Notes _____

_____

Menu Notes _____

_____

Proprietor's Autograph _____

TEA PLACE 19 _____

Scrapbook Memories

TEA VIEWS 19

TEACUP RATING

1 2 3 4 5

Date / /

OVERALL RATING: 1 - 5 TEACUPS WITH 5 BEING EXCEPTIONAL.

Tea Shop

Proprietor

Location

Companions

Tea Names and Types

Tea Tasting Notes

Menu Notes

Proprietor's Autograph

TEA PLACE 20 _____

Scrapbook Memories

Tea Views 20

Teacup Rating

1 2 3 4 5

$Date$ ___/___/___

OVERALL RATING: 1 - 5 TEACUPS WITH 5 BEING EXCEPTIONAL.

$Tea Shop$ _____

$Proprietor$ _____

$Location$ _____

$Companions$ _____

$Tea Names and Types$ _____

$Tea Tasting Notes$ _____

_____

$Menu Notes$ _____

_____

$Proprietor's Autograph$ _____

TEA PLACE 21 _____

Scrapbook Memories

TEA VIEWS 21

TEACUP RATING

1   2   3   4   5

OVERALL RATING: 1 - 5 TEACUPS WITH 5 BEING EXCEPTIONAL.

*D*ate / /

*T*ea *S*hop

*P*roprietor

*L*ocation

*C*ompanions

*T*ea *N*ames and *T*ypes

*T*ea *T*asting *N*otes

*M*enu *N*otes

*P*roprietor's *A*utograph

TEA PLACE 22 _____

Scrapbook Memories

TEA VIEWS 22

TEACUP RATING

1 2 3 4 5

OVERALL RATING: 1 - 5 TEACUPS WITH 5 BEING EXCEPTIONAL.

$Date$ ___/___/___

$Tea Shop$ _____

$Proprietor$ _____

$Location$ _____

$Companions$ _____

$Tea Names and Types$ _____

$Tea Tasting Notes$ _____

_____

$Menu Notes$ _____

_____

$Proprietor's Autograph$ _____

TEA PLACE 23 _____

Scrapbook Memories

TEA VIEWS 23

TEACUP RATING

1 2 3 4 5

*D*ate ___/ /___

OVERALL RATING: 1 - 5 TEACUPS WITH 5 BEING EXCEPTIONAL.

*T*ea *S*hop _____

*P*roprietor _____

*L*ocation _____

*C*ompanions _____

*T*ea *N*ames and *T*ypes _____

*T*ea *T*asting *N*otes _____

_____

*M*enu *N*otes _____

_____

*P*roprietor's *A*utograph _____

TEA PLACE 24 _____

Scrapbook Memories

TEA VIEWS 24

TEACUP RATING

1 2 3 4 5

OVERALL RATING: 1 - 5 TEACUPS WITH 5 BEING EXCEPTIONAL.

$\mathcal{D}$ate _____ / / _____

$\mathcal{T}$ea $\mathcal{S}$hop _____

$\mathcal{P}$roprietor _____

$\mathcal{L}$ocation _____

$\mathcal{C}$ompanions _____

$\mathcal{T}$ea $\mathcal{N}$ames and $\mathcal{T}$ypes _____

$\mathcal{T}$ea $\mathcal{T}$asting $\mathcal{N}$otes _____

_____

$\mathcal{M}$enu $\mathcal{N}$otes _____

_____

$\mathcal{P}$roprietor's $\mathcal{A}$utograph _____

TEA PLACE 25 _____

Scrapbook Memories

TEA VIEWS 25

TEACUP RATING

1 2 3 4 5

OVERALL RATING: 1 - 5 TEACUPS WITH 5 BEING EXCEPTIONAL.

Date ___ / ___ / ___

Tea Shop _____

Proprietor _____

Location _____

Companions _____

Tea Names and Types _____

Tea Tasting Notes _____

_____

Menu Notes _____

_____

Proprietor's Autograph _____

TEA PLACE 26 _____

Scrapbook Memories

TEA VIEWS 26

TEACUP RATING

1 2 3 4 5

OVERALL RATING: 1 - 5 TEACUPS WITH 5 BEING EXCEPTIONAL.

$\mathcal{D}$ate ___/___/___

$\mathcal{T}$ea $\mathcal{S}$hop _____

$\mathcal{P}$roprietor _____

$\mathcal{L}$ocation _____

$\mathcal{C}$ompanions _____

$\mathcal{T}$ea $\mathcal{N}$ames and $\mathcal{T}$ypes _____

$\mathcal{T}$ea $\mathcal{T}$asting $\mathcal{N}$otes _____

_____

$\mathcal{M}$enu $\mathcal{N}$otes _____

_____

$\mathcal{P}$roprietor's $\mathcal{A}$utograph _____

TEA PLACE 27 _____

Scrapbook Memories

TEA VIEWS 27

TEACUP RATING

| 1 | 2 | 3 | 4 | 5 |

$\mathscr{D}$ate _____ / / _____

OVERALL RATING: 1 - 5 TEACUPS WITH 5 BEING EXCEPTIONAL.

$\mathscr{T}$ea $\mathscr{S}$hop _____

$\mathscr{P}$roprietor _____

$\mathscr{L}$ocation _____

$\mathscr{C}$ompanions _____

$\mathscr{T}$ea $\mathscr{N}$ames and $\mathscr{T}$ypes _____

$\mathscr{T}$ea $\mathscr{T}$asting $\mathscr{N}$otes _____

_____

$\mathscr{M}$enu $\mathscr{N}$otes _____

_____

$\mathscr{P}$roprietor's $\mathscr{A}$utograph _____

TEA PLACE 28 _____

Scrapbook Memories

TEA VIEWS 28

TEACUP RATING

1 2 3 4 5

OVERALL RATING: 1 - 5 TEACUPS WITH 5 BEING EXCEPTIONAL.

Date ___ / / ___

Tea Shop _____

Proprietor _____

Location _____

Companions _____

Tea Names and Types _____

Tea Tasting Notes _____

_____

Menu Notes _____

_____

Proprietor's Autograph _____

TEA PLACE 29 _____

Scrapbook Memories

TEA VIEWS 29

TEACUP RATING

1 2 3 4 5

OVERALL RATING: 1 - 5 TEACUPS WITH 5 BEING EXCEPTIONAL.

D_{ate} _____ / / _____

T_{ea} S_{hop} _____

$P_{roprietor}$ _____

$L_{ocation}$ _____

$C_{ompanions}$ _____

T_{ea} $N_{ames and}$ T_{ypes} _____

T_{ea} T_{asting} N_{otes} _____

_____

M_{enu} N_{otes} _____

_____

$P_{roprietor's}$ $A_{utograph}$ _____

TEA PLACE 30 _____

Scrapbook Memories

TEA VIEWS 30

TEACUP RATING

1 2 3 4 5

OVERALL RATING: 1 - 5 TEACUPS WITH 5 BEING EXCEPTIONAL.

$\mathcal{D}$ate _____ / / _____

$\mathcal{T}$ea $\mathcal{S}$hop _____

$\mathcal{P}$roprietor _____

$\mathcal{L}$ocation _____

$\mathcal{C}$ompanions _____

$\mathcal{T}$ea $\mathcal{N}$ames and $\mathcal{T}$ypes _____

$\mathcal{T}$ea $\mathcal{T}$asting $\mathcal{N}$otes _____

_____

$\mathcal{M}$enu $\mathcal{N}$otes _____

_____

$\mathcal{P}$roprietor's $\mathcal{A}$utograph _____

Tea Place 31 _____

Scrapbook Memories

TEA VIEWS 31

TEACUP RATING

1 2 3 4 5

Date ___ / ___ / ___

OVERALL RATING: 1 - 5 TEACUPS WITH 5 BEING EXCEPTIONAL.

Tea Shop _____

Proprietor _____

Location _____

Companions _____

Tea Names and Types _____

Tea Tasting Notes _____

_____

Menu Notes _____

_____

Proprietor's Autograph _____

TEA PLACE 32 _____

Scrapbook Memories

TEA VIEWS 32

TEACUP RATING

1 2 3 4 5

OVERALL RATING: 1 - 5 TEACUPS WITH 5 BEING EXCEPTIONAL.

Date _____ / / _____

Tea Shop _____

Proprietor _____

Location _____

Companions _____

Tea Names and Types _____

Tea Tasting Notes _____

_____

Menu Notes _____

_____

Proprietor's Autograph _____

TEA PLACE 33 _____

Scrapbook Memories

TEA VIEWS 33

TEACUP RATING

1   2   3   4   5

OVERALL RATING: 1 - 5 TEACUPS WITH 5 BEING EXCEPTIONAL.

Date _____/_____/_____

Tea Shop _____

Proprietor _____

Location _____

Companions _____

Tea Names and Types _____

Tea Tasting Notes _____

_____

Menu Notes _____

_____

Proprietor's Autograph _____

TEA PLACE 34 _____

Scrapbook Memories

TEA VIEWS 34

TEACUP RATING

1   2   3   4   5

OVERALL RATING: 1 - 5 TEACUPS WITH 5 BEING EXCEPTIONAL.

Date ___/___/___

Tea Shop _____

Proprietor _____

Location _____

Companions _____

Tea Names and Types _____

Tea Tasting Notes _____

_____

Menu Notes _____

_____

Proprietor's Autograph _____

TEA PLACE 35 _____

Scrapbook Memories

TEA VIEWS 35

TEACUP RATING

1   2   3   4   5

OVERALL RATING: 1 - 5 TEACUPS WITH 5 BEING EXCEPTIONAL.

Date ___/___/___

Tea Shop _____

Proprietor _____

Location _____

Companions _____

Tea Names and Types _____

Tea Tasting Notes _____

_____

Menu Notes _____

_____

Proprietor's Autograph _____

TEA PLACE 36 _____

Scrapbook Memories

TEA VIEWS 36

TEACUP RATING

1 2 3 4 5

OVERALL RATING: 1 - 5 TEACUPS WITH 5 BEING EXCEPTIONAL.

$\mathscr{D}$ate _____ / / _____

$\mathscr{T}$ea $\mathscr{S}$hop _____

$\mathscr{P}$roprietor _____

$\mathscr{L}$ocation _____

$\mathscr{C}$ompanions _____

$\mathscr{T}$ea $\mathscr{N}$ames and $\mathscr{T}$ypes _____

$\mathscr{T}$ea $\mathscr{T}$asting $\mathscr{N}$otes _____

_____

$\mathscr{M}$enu $\mathscr{N}$otes _____

_____

$\mathscr{P}$roprietor's $\mathscr{A}$utograph _____

TEA PLACE 37 _____

Scrapbook Memories

TEA VIEWS 37

TEACUP RATING

1 2 3 4 5

OVERALL RATING: 1 - 5 TEACUPS WITH 5 BEING EXCEPTIONAL.

Date ____ / / ____

Tea Shop _____

Proprietor _____

Location _____

Companions _____

Tea Names and Types _____

Tea Tasting Notes _____

_____

Menu Notes _____

_____

Proprietor's Autograph _____

TEA PLACE 38 _____

Scrapbook Memories

TEA VIEWS 38

TEACUP RATING

OVERALL RATING: 1 - 5 TEACUPS WITH 5 BEING EXCEPTIONAL.

$\mathcal{D}$ate _____ / / _____

$\mathcal{T}$ea $\mathcal{S}$hop

$\mathcal{P}$roprietor

$\mathcal{L}$ocation

$\mathcal{C}$ompanions

$\mathcal{T}$ea $\mathcal{N}$ames and $\mathcal{T}$ypes

$\mathcal{T}$ea $\mathcal{T}$asting $\mathcal{N}$otes

$\mathcal{M}$enu $\mathcal{N}$otes

$\mathcal{P}$roprietor's $\mathcal{A}$utograph

TEA PLACE 39 _____

Scrapbook Memories

TEA VIEWS 39

TEACUP RATING

1 2 3 4 5

OVERALL RATING: 1 - 5 TEACUPS WITH 5 BEING EXCEPTIONAL.

Date _ / /_____

Tea Shop _____

Proprietor _____

Location _____

Companions _____

Tea Names and Types _____

Tea Tasting Notes _____

_____

Menu Notes _____

_____

Proprietor's Autograph _____

TEA PLACE 40 _____

Scrapbook Memories

TEA VIEWS 40

TEACUP RATING

1   2   3   4   5

$Date$ ___ / ___ / ___

OVERALL RATING: 1 - 5 TEACUPS WITH 5 BEING EXCEPTIONAL.

$Tea Shop$ _____

$Proprietor$ _____

$Location$ _____

$Companions$ _____

$Tea Names and Types$ _____

$Tea Tasting Notes$ _____

_____

$Menu Notes$ _____

_____

$Proprietor's Autograph$ _____

TEA PLACE 41 _____

Scrapbook Memories

TEA VIEWS 41

TEACUP RATING

1 2 3 4 5

OVERALL RATING: 1 - 5 TEACUPS WITH 5 BEING EXCEPTIONAL.

$Date$ ___ / / ___

$Tea Shop$ _____

$Proprietor$ _____

$Location$ _____

$Companions$ _____

$Tea Names and Types$ _____

$Tea Tasting Notes$ _____

_____

$Menu Notes$ _____

_____

$Proprietor's Autograph$ _____

TEA PLACE 42 _____

Scrapbook Memories

TEA VIEWS 42

TEACUP RATING

1 2 3 4 5

OVERALL RATING: 1 - 5 TEACUPS WITH 5 BEING EXCEPTIONAL.

*D*ate _____ / / _____

*T*ea *S*hop _____

*P*roprietor _____

*L*ocation _____

*C*ompanions _____

*T*ea *N*ames and *T*ypes _____

*T*ea *T*asting *N*otes _____

_____

*M*enu *N*otes _____

_____

*P*roprietor's *A*utograph _____

TEA PLACE 43 _____

Scrapbook Memories

TEA VIEWS 43

TEACUP RATING

1 2 3 4 5

OVERALL RATING: 1 - 5 TEACUPS WITH 5 BEING EXCEPTIONAL.

Date ___/___/___

Tea Shop _____

Proprietor _____

Location _____

Companions _____

Tea Names and Types _____

Tea Tasting Notes _____

_____

Menu Notes _____

_____

Proprietor's Autograph _____

TEA PLACE 44 _____

Scrapbook Memories

TEA VIEWS 44

TEACUP RATING

1 2 3 4 5

Date ___/___/___

OVERALL RATING: 1 - 5 TEACUPS WITH 5 BEING EXCEPTIONAL.

Tea Shop _____

Proprietor _____

Location _____

Companions _____

Tea Names and Types _____

Tea Tasting Notes _____

_____

Menu Notes _____

_____

Proprietor's Autograph _____

TEA PLACE 45 _____

Scrapbook Memories

TEA VIEWS 45

1 2 3 4 5

$\mathcal{D}$ate / /

OVERALL RATING: 1 - 5 TEACUPS WITH 5 BEING EXCEPTIONAL.

$\mathcal{T}$ea $\mathcal{S}$hop

$\mathcal{P}$roprietor

$\mathcal{L}$ocation

$\mathcal{C}$ompanions

$\mathcal{T}$ea $\mathcal{N}$ames and $\mathcal{T}$ypes

$\mathcal{T}$ea $\mathcal{T}$asting $\mathcal{N}$otes

$\mathcal{M}$enu $\mathcal{N}$otes

$\mathcal{P}$roprietor's $\mathcal{A}$utograph

TEA PLACE 46 _____

Scrapbook Memories

TEA VIEWS 46

TEACUP RATING

1 2 3 4 5

*D*ate ___ / / ___

OVERALL RATING: 1 - 5 TEACUPS WITH 5 BEING EXCEPTIONAL.

*T*ea *S*hop

*P*roprietor

*L*ocation

*C*ompanions

*T*ea *N*ames and *T*ypes

*T*ea *T*asting *N*otes

*M*enu *N*otes

*P*roprietor's *A*utograph

TEA PLACE 47 _____

Scrapbook Memories

TEA VIEWS 47

TEACUP RATING

1 2 3 4 5

OVERALL RATING: 1 - 5 TEACUPS WITH 5 BEING EXCEPTIONAL.

Date ___/___/___

Tea Shop _____

Proprietor _____

Location _____

Companions _____

Tea Names and Types _____

Tea Tasting Notes _____

_____

Menu Notes _____

_____

Proprietor's Autograph _____

TEA PLACE 48 _____

Scrapbook Memories

TEA VIEWS 48

TEACUP RATING

1 2 3 4 5

$\mathcal{D}$ate _/_/_

OVERALL RATING: 1 - 5 TEACUPS WITH 5 BEING EXCEPTIONAL.

$\mathcal{T}$ea $\mathcal{S}$hop ___

$\mathcal{P}$roprietor ___

$\mathcal{L}$ocation ___

$\mathcal{C}$ompanions ___

$\mathcal{T}$ea $\mathcal{N}$ames and $\mathcal{T}$ypes ___

$\mathcal{T}$ea $\mathcal{T}$asting $\mathcal{N}$otes ___

___

$\mathcal{M}$enu $\mathcal{N}$otes ___

___

$\mathcal{P}$roprietor's $\mathcal{A}$utograph ___

TEA PLACE 49 _____

Scrapbook Memories

TEA VIEWS 49

TEACUP RATING

1 2 3 4 5

$\mathcal{D}$ate   / /

OVERALL RATING: 1 - 5 TEACUPS WITH 5 BEING EXCEPTIONAL.

$\mathcal{T}$ea $\mathcal{S}$hop

$\mathcal{P}$roprietor

$\mathcal{L}$ocation

$\mathcal{C}$ompanions

$\mathcal{T}$ea $\mathcal{N}$ames and $\mathcal{T}$ypes

$\mathcal{T}$ea $\mathcal{T}$asting $\mathcal{N}$otes

$\mathcal{M}$enu $\mathcal{N}$otes

$\mathcal{P}$roprietor's $\mathcal{A}$utograph

TEA PLACE 50 _____

Scrapbook Memories

TEA VIEWS 50

TEACUP RATING

1 2 3 4 5

OVERALL RATING: 1 - 5 TEACUPS WITH 5 BEING EXCEPTIONAL.

*D*ate _____/____/_____

*T*ea *S*hop

*P*roprietor

*L*ocation

*C*ompanions

*T*ea *N*ames and *T*ypes

*T*ea *T*asting *N*otes

*M*enu *N*otes

*P*roprietor's *A*utograph

TEA PLACE 51 _____

Scrapbook Memories

TEA VIEWS 51

TEACUP RATING

1   2   3   4   5

OVERALL RATING: 1 - 5 TEACUPS WITH 5 BEING EXCEPTIONAL.

$Date$ ___ / ___ / ___

$Tea Shop$ _____

$Proprietor$ _____

$Location$ _____

$Companions$ _____

$Tea Names and Types$ _____

$Tea Tasting Notes$ _____

_____

$Menu Notes$ _____

_____

$Proprietor's Autograph$ _____

TEA PLACE 52 _____

Scrapbook Memories

TEA VIEWS 52

TEACUP RATING

1 2 3 4 5

*D*ate / /

OVERALL RATING: 1 - 5 TEACUPS WITH 5 BEING EXCEPTIONAL.

*T*ea *S*hop

*P*roprietor

*L*ocation

*C*ompanions

*T*ea *N*ames and *T*ypes

*T*ea *T*asting *N*otes

*M*enu *N*otes

*P*roprietor's *A*utograph

Thank you for purchasing Tea Journal – A Tea Lover's Diary! I hope you enjoy every tea-filled page!

Remember, Tea Journal will make a great gift basket item, tea society journal or "just because" gift!

~ Jennifer

RECOMMENDED READING

Other Books by Jennifer C. Petersen

Available on Amazon in print and Kindle:
http://www.amazon.com/Jennifer-C.-Petersen

17-76 Tea Party Award Winning Recipes
    17 Jam and Scone Recipes
    76 Scone Recipes
    Bonus Recipes!
    Foreword by James Norwood Pratt
    Reviews by Judith Krall-Russo, Pat Jollota and Pat Stephens
Lavender Cookbook: Essential Lavender Recipes
Lavender Cookbook: Simple & Delicious Recipes
A Colonial Tea – an historical one-act play
Scone Recipes: Amazing Scone Baking Race – Delicious, Prize-winning Scone Recipes

Certified Tea Education Classes:

Tea Council of the USA
Tea Council of Canada
Tea Council of the UK
Tea Business School

ABOUT THE AUTHOR

Jennifer Petersen, Tea Trade Mart, is a tea enthusiast with over 18 years as a tea blender, retail/wholesale business, and tea restaurant & gift shop owner . She is the owner and director of Tea Business School.

A supporting member of STI since APTI (American Premium Tea Institute) and ST*R combined to become STI, Ms. Petersen is a professional speaker and trainer recommended by the Specialty Tea Institute. She is a frequent speaker at international coffee and tea events and trade shows.

She is currently serving her third term on the STI Advisory Board and chaired the 2005 STI Tea Symposium in Seattle, Washington. She is co-chair of the STI Education Committee and serves on the marketing committee.

She is a member of the Specialty Tea Institute, Mid Atlantic Tea Business Association, Hawaii Tea Society, National Association of Christian Women Entrepreneurs and Women Entrepreneurs Organization.

Printed in Great Britain
by Amazon